BELLA IN
WYCH-ELM

ANDREW SPARKE

APS PUBLICATIONS

APS Publications,
4 Oakleigh Road,
Stourbridge,
West Midlands,
DY8 2JX

www.andrewsparke.com

CONTENTS

INTRODUCTION

This short book draws together all the theories about Bella, a local cause célèbre in the part of Worcestershire bordering the Black Country, an area to the West of Birmingham encompassing the modern boroughs of Dudley, Sandwell and Walsall and the city of Wolverhampton. Her body, or the skeletal remains of it were discovered in 1943, hidden in a hollow tree in Hagley Woods, sparking a mystery which abides to this day.

Writing nearly eighty years later, it's clear that the main reason for the enduring power of Bella's story is that it remains an unsolved murder, involving a bizarre means of disposal, with the victim's identity and the means of her death remaining unascertainable. The only person who can be sure of Bella's actual identity is her murderer who must by now have taken his or her secret to the grave.

This is a work about how folklore and legend take over when forensic evidence is lacking but it's published alongside another book by my friend Pete Merrill's young son Alex which promises to be a turning point in Bella's story and must be read by anyone who's fascination is sparked by the case history as I've been able to outline it. What Alex has done is to explore the crime scene and forensic reports from modern first principles and his theory about the timing and nature of Bella's death and the likely errors of supposition and consequent mis-description of Bella are fascinating. His true genius though has been to procure the scientific recreation of Bella's face and thus enable a new search to start for Bella in family photographic archives.

In issuing this book in a new edition I have referenced Alex's discoveries but if you want to see Bella's face for yourself then you'll need to get his book *Who Put Bella In The Wych Elm? Vol.1 The Crime Scene Revisited* and who knows what revelations *Vol.2* will bring.

For now, this is the story of *Hagley Woods Bella* as it has evolved between 1943 and the present day.

Andrew Sparke
February 2018

FIRST QUESTIONS

The questions the case raises are innumerable. Among the more obvious are the following:

Who was Bella?
How did she die?
Was she murdered and if so who killed her?
Why did nobody report her missing?
How did she get to the wood?
Why was she put in the tree?
As rumours at the time had it, was she a prostitute, a gypsy or a Nazi spy?
Did she just fall foul of a husband or lover?
How did the story of a severed hand arise?
How did her remains come to disappear?

What happened to her child or children?
What does her case file with the West Mercia Police contain?
Why has so much of the documentation associated with the investigation of her murder missing?
Is there an MI5 aspect?
Why is this case still a mystery nearly eighty years after it happened?

The thing is that most of these questions are unanswered, and at this remove, unanswerable, making *Bella in the Wych-Elm* an enduring folk legend and a fertile ground for conspiracy theories. No wonder the case still attracts such levels of interest today.

DISCOVERING THE CORPSE

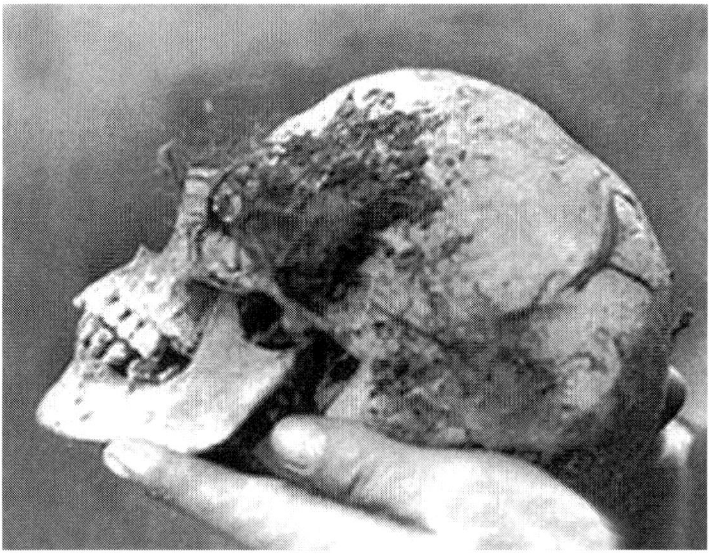

People disappear. Even in a world as well regulated as we like to believe ours to be. In this country we continue to see the evidence of that in the form of *Missing Persons* posters and media coverage of unsolved murders, each one a minor tragedy or mystery in the making. Even so, in England it's still true that only a minority of killings remain unsolved and few victims remain unidentified, which means the case of Bella is doubly unusual.

The story of Bella is bookended by the actions of young people. It only came to light at all because of young men roaming around, poking their noses into places an adult might never bother to look. Writing nearly eighty years later, it's teenagers who are keeping the story alive, scrawling slogans on walls, being cool or amusing themselves, meaning nothing serious by it. Mind you, that assumes the ongoing graffiti is the work of teenage pranksters.

To get behind the modern iteration of a local legend with supernatural elements, we need to go all the way back to April 18th

1943 and deep into the Hagley Woods, which run alongside the main road between Birmingham and Kidderminster. We may be in the middle of a world war but here in the countryside, apart from rationing and the excitement of aircraft overhead, straying from the conflict raging over Birmingham, Wolverhampton and Coventry's industrial heart, the daily lives of children and young people are little changed; they're still bored by schoolwork and itching to be out doing stuff in the fresh air. They have an additional motivation in the desire to supplement their food rations with purloined eggs and rabbits and scrumped apples.

Tonight, at dusk, Fred Payne, Bob Farmer, Thomas Willetts and Robert Hart, accompanied by their three lurcher dogs, Trix, Jock and Nigger, having failed to flush out any rabbits, are raiding birds' nests, trespassing on Lord Cobham's estate. Clambering around an old Wych-Hazel tree (not a Wych-Elm although that's how it's going to be characterised). Robert Hart finds he can see, down in the hollowed-out tree trunk, about four feet off the ground, what appear to be animal bones. He calls his friends over and Bob Farmer reaches down to pull it out. He can't get at it and so finds a stick and hoiks it out, getting the shock of his life when a human skull bounces at his feet. With its empty eye sockets and derailed lower teeth, it still carries a hank of hair and scraps of flesh, unconsumed by vermin, clinging to the forehead. The others gather around to look at it; to poke it and discuss what to do with it. A lot of false bravado prevails and they want to show Fred's older brother, but, given the illicit nature of their expedition into the woods, the decision is taken to put the skull back where it came from. They return home in a spirit of high adventure with something new to boast about to their mates.

The secret doesn't hold. Tommy Willetts is very affected by what he's seen. His father asks what's up with him and his son spills the beans, dumping a wholly unexpected problem in his father's lap. Once he's convinced Tommy is telling the truth, he has no choice but to call the police, which means contacting a local Police

Sergeant, Chris Lambourne. On the following day, April 19th, Lambourne rousts out Bob Hart and uses him as a guide to find the hollow tree.

Sergeant Skerratt

Next on the scene is Sergeant Richard Skerratt from Clent with Constable Jack Pound from Hagley and Sergeant Jack Wheeler. It will be the next day before detectives and specialist forensic support can get there from Worcester and the scene of the crime has to be protected. Volunteers are sought and Special Constable William Eric Douglas-Osborn takes on the doubtless unnerving task of guarding the tree overnight.

On the 20th April Detective Superintendent Sidney Inight arrives to take charge. The crime scene is accessible from the unnamed track we now know as Hagley Wood Lane. Inight brings with him Deputy Inspector Thomas Williams and Professor James Webster, Head of the Home Office Forensic Science Laboratory, newly established at Birmingham University.

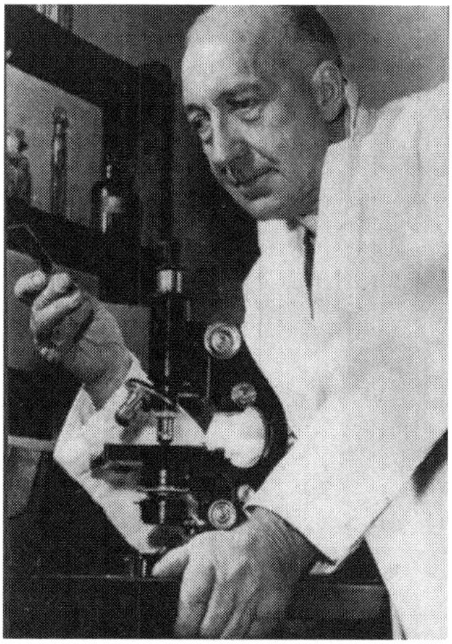

Professor James Webster

The new arrivals rapidly discover the entrance into the hollow tree trunk is too narrow to permit the examination they need to make of the body in situ. An axe is rapidly procured and Jack Pound splits the tree open for them. Jammed down inside, feet first, are the bones of the woman we have come to know as Bella.

The wood itself is subject to an intensive search using special constables, Home Guard personnel, servicemen on leave, Boy Scouts and other volunteers. Boys from Stourbridge's Grange School are offered sixpence apiece to join the search and half a crown for any human bone they find. They don't find much; a green bottle and a pair of size 5 1/2, midnight- blue shoes. It will later be alleged that some thirteen paces from the hollow tree, the severed bones of a small right hand were discovered but this seems to be a later invention.

At some point the volunteers are de-briefed and make formal statements about what they did on 19th and 20th April. In the fullness of time those statements are lodged for safekeeping at the Worcestershire County Records Office. Sometime during the 1950s the files are mislaid or stolen, never to be seen again. Unfortunately, missing and uncollected evidence is to dog this case almost from its inception. Even the skeleton itself will eventually disappear.

The purported tree as published in contemporary newspapers

The actual tree in Hagley Wood from crime scene photographs

THE FORENSICS

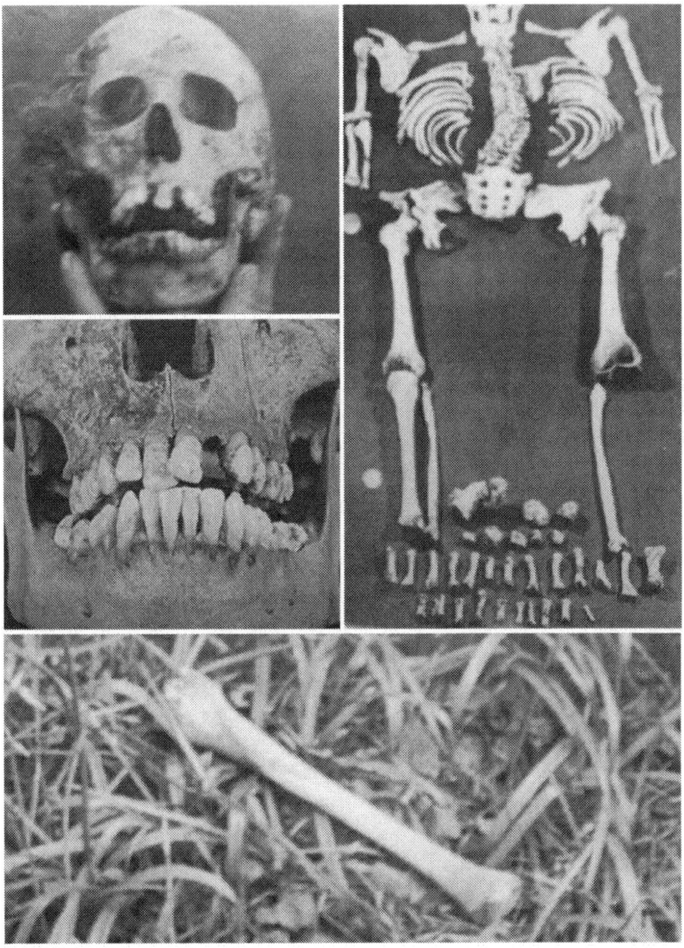

The Worcestershire County Police can't help speculating. They don't have anything much to go on at all. What comes out of the hollow tree are skeletal remains and fragments of rotten clothing. The skeleton is in fact almost complete. What's still missing are a few smaller bones and two of the teeth.

Still, if Professor Webster can't crack the secrets of this death, nobody can. He states as his belief that the skeleton is of a woman, five feet tall, aged about thirty-five and certainly neither older than forty nor younger than twenty-five. Her pelvic bones tell him she's probably had at least one child. She has mid-brown hair and a noticeable irregularity of the front teeth. She has a cheap wedding ring of rolled gold worth no more than half a crown on her finger. The professor says from the wear and patina she's worn it for four years or so. And she's been dead for eighteen months at least but no more than three years, meaning the latest date of death is October 1941 and even the earliest possible date is late 1940. In all probability, she died between April and October of 1941.

In part Professor Webster may be unconciously influenced in setting his parameters for the likely date of death by reference to the shoes discovered in Hagley Woods at the time the body was recovered. We will see that that may be an error which misdirects the enquiry.

Another element of possible mis-direction of the police arises from the tests in use in the 1940s to ascertain probable height from measurement of the long bones of the legs. When Professor Webster states she was five feet tall, he is applying current professional knowledge but if he isn't right on that score (and modern hindsight will come up with a different result), then the police may unwittingly eliminate from their enquiries a number of women reported missing prior to 1943, any one of whom might in fact be Bella.

Professor Webster can find no clear signs of disease or violence but stuffed into the skull is a strip of rotting taffeta which he speculates may indicate asphyxiation as the cause of death. He is unaware that the fabric may have been lodged there only as a consequence of Bob Farmer poking the skull with his stick. It's only later when the lads are re-questioned that they admit that the fabric may have been jammed in as they levered the skull out of the tree.

The recovered fragments of clothing are analysed and revealed to be summer-weight garments including underwear and there are no signs of the buttons or material that could come from a coat. It seems Bella died in warmer months.

Bella's clothes are identified as a mustard-coloured woollen skirt, of good quality material and with a side-zip, and a blue and yellow striped, knitted cardigan with a light blue belt, worn over underwear, which to some extent reduces the possibility that Bella was actively working as a prostitute at the time of her death. Her underwear comprises a peach or fawn coloured taffeta underskirt (of cheap, hand-sewn material), a corset identified from residual fragments and the metal stays, and a cheap pair of navy blue cotton knickers. Professor Webster states that she was not wearing stockings because otherwise some of the cotton should have survived.

Essentially all the police have to go on is a speculative recreation from scraps of Bella's clothing, and the belief that she was five feet tall, aged in her thirties and, if the shoes recovered at the scene are hers, that she had size 5 1/2 feet; all linked to the supposition that she disappeared and died late in 1941 or early in 1942.

INVESTIGATING MURDER

The investigation may be hampered by lack of concrete evidence but it's reportedly thorough enough. Armed with Professor Webster's findings, the Worcestershire Police plough through over 3,000 reports of missing women across the whole country and draw a blank. The unidentified woman, matches the description of nobody logged as a missing person by any other police force.

Bella's teeth might be expected to yield her identity. The irregular front teeth and a missing tooth, recently extracted, from the lower right side of her mouth are distinctive enough. Details are circulated to the newspapers and go to every registered dentist in England but again, no joy, although it's fair to point out that there are probably many unregistered dental practitioners in Britain at the time.

The search of the area around the hollow tree turns up a woman's identity card but at the address stated on it the presumed victim is discovered alive and well, if baffled as to how her identity card could have ended up in Hagley Woods, a place she says she's never been.

In the area, the belief is that the murderer must have local knowledge; few think anybody could just stumble on the hollow tree in the dark woods as a place to hide a body.

The green bottle found at the scene affords no further lead but the women's shoes are a different matter. Professor Webster's opinion is that "...it would appear probable that the pair of shoes, one recovered from the bole of the tree, and the other at some distance are connected with this body." They are, therefore deemed worthy of investigative effort. This is a surprising conclusion given that small women commonly have small feet and that the shoes when discovered are separate from the corpse and contain neither foot nor ankle bones inside them.

Eventually the shoe's manufacturer is tracked down. Six thousand pairs were made and the owners of all of them are traced except for six pairs sold to unknown customers from a Dudley market stall. This is another dead end although not before a colossal amount of effort has determined that the shoes were manufactured about 1940 and are of a dark blue colour in a style known in the trade as 'Black Leather Gibsons'. They have three rows of pin punchings in the uppers and crepe soles and heels. The size is confirmed as 5 1/2 and the shoe uppers are stamped with the maker's designation D.956. They aren't cheap shoes – an identical shoe retailed at 13s/11d in 1940 – but they are well worn.

The deceased's clothing might have been expected to yield further clues but doesn't, given the lack of surviving labels in them despite there being enough rotting fragments of the rest of her clothes to describe them with some hope of accuracy. Were the labels deliberately cut out or were Bella's clothes all bought as seconds from a market? It's another unusual feature of the case which is never answered.

There's an inquest of course. On the 28th April 1943 the Stourbridge coroner returns a verdict of murder 'by person or persons unknown' and accepts asphyxiation as the probable cause of death. He suggests on the balance of probabilities that the body was stuffed into the hollow tree when it was still warm. He accepts Professor Webster's reasoning that it couldn't have been done once rigor mortis set in. He presumably dismisses as unlikely that it was done after a few days delay once the processes of putrefaction relaxed the body when it would have been a far less pleasant task and because she would need to have been hidden in the interim.

The possibility that she was killed elsewhere, allowed to rot and only hidden in the Wych Hazel tree much later is either never addressed or dismissed out of hand because the shoes assumed to be hers were only manufactured in 1940; ergo Bella cannot have died before then.

The trail goes cold. Nobody knows or is telling anything. We can't find out who she is or where she comes from, let alone who killed her.

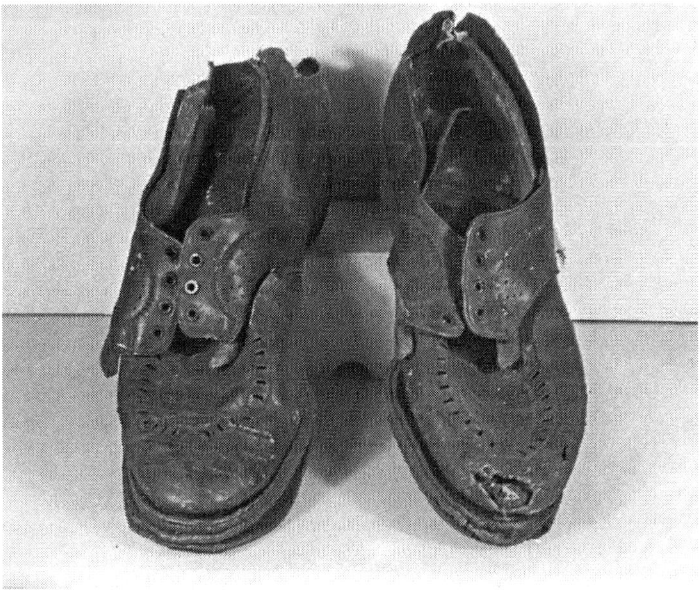

THE BELLA MESSAGES

Six months later, in the autumn of 1943, a spate of local wall-daubing occurs. Taunting the police is hardly a new phenomenon. Sometimes it spurs on an investigation; at other times it obstructs and side-tracks effort, as with the notorious *I'm Jack* calls which dogged the hunt for the Yorkshire Ripper. The graffiti in the Old Hill area reads *Who put Luebeller down the Wych-Elm?* written in chalk on a wall using capital letters, three inches in height. As the message is repeated in other locations in Birmingham and the Black Country, it changes slightly with time, like a Chinese whisper, becoming *Who put Bella in the witch elm* or referring to *Hagley Wood Bella.*

The name is interesting though. If it had been Bella from the beginning, it might be shrugged off as an example of a Black Country usage indicating affection, much as Italians might use it. But *Luebella* is specific; an unlikely choice out of the blue. It might be an indicator or clue; or the opposite, an attempt to deceive or mislead. But either way the graffiti suggests somebody who knows something about the victim feels driven to communicate. Not that this gives the police any joy because there is still nobody who fits the profile of the woman's body from the Wych-Hazel tree who has a name like Luebella or any variant of Bella, such as Clarabelle or Isabella, among the manila folders containing the missing person files.

The graffiti isn't the only response from the public which diverts precious police attention away from the pressing business of investigating Bella's case. There is a spate of letters, either mischievous in nature or claiming various missing persons as the unidentified victim. Among them are names which have to be checked, such as Ann Forrest and Bella Luer and Bella Tonks, as well as people whose names are concocted and entirely fictitious. Among the correspondence is a reference to an Anabella but that's in an anonymous letter with nothing else helpful to say.

None of the leads turns out to be anything other than a red herring; either the named person turns up or is too young or too tall to be our Bella. And time is passing.

RETROSPECTIVE EVIDENCE

In July 1941 an executive from a local industrial concern telephones the police to report hearing a woman's screams coming from Hagley Woods. A schoolteacher walking nearby hears them too. Sergeant Skerratt and Constable Pound search the area and find nothing. This is some twenty months before Bella's body is found in the hollow tree but remembering this in 1943 adds nothing significant to the investigation.

One possible identification of Bella is provided much later in time by Warwick Plant, the son of the publican of The Crown in Brierley Hill High Street. His mother befriends a small woman who has come in asking to be allowed to play the piano and sing for coppers. The woman gives her name as Bella and says before the war she used to be in a concert party touring Europe but packed up and came back to Britain when the war broke out. She also says she sings in another pub, The Mitre in Stourbridge. Mrs Plant ends up giving Bella a pair of two-tone, crepe-soled shoes to wear to replace the other woman's shoes which are down at heel and have holes in their soles.

Subsequently from a bus, Warwick claims he saw her working with a man in a field near Hagley Wood.

The mystery woman comes into the pub several times after that but on her last visit arrives with bruises and a black eye dealt her, Bella says, by her landlord – she lives in Birmingham Street on the edge of Stourbridge.

She doesn't return after that and although Warwick is sent by his mother to The Mitre a couple of times to find her, he fails in that endeavour, spotting only the rough-looking man he once saw Bella with and doesn't dare approach for fear of receiving a thumping. Bella is never seen again.

Warwick joins the RAF soon afterwards and doesn't learn of the Hagley Woods discovery until he's home on leave in 1944 and his sister, after discussing the Daily Sketch coverage of the case with him, goes to the police. It isn't followed up and Warwick Plant is never interviewed.

Perhaps neither matter nor the reporting of bad smells in the vicinity of the tree in Hagley Wood and nearby gypsy encampment, are relevant to the mystery of Bella at all but those who report these events clearly believe they might be.

What the police do have on file is an incident report, from around the time Bella must have been killed, of a car parking up one evening on the roadside near Hagley Woods with a uniformed RAF officer in the driving seat and a young woman, apparently asleep on the back seat, covered by a coat.

The report is filed by a member of the Home guard in 1941 called Basterfield. He's patrolling for enemy parachutists and approaches the car in the layby. Spotting the woman lying on the back seat under a coat, he goes round to the driver's side of the car. The driver holds up his warrant card for Basterfield to see and is instructed to move off.

Whether this is the dying Bella or not we may never know.

WITCHCRAFT

Human beings can't abide uncertainty. If there's a vacuum of knowledge we rush to fill it with speculation and if there's still a gap then a supernatural explanation is never far away. Enter onto the scene, an influential anthropologist and archaeologist with a strong leaning towards the occult. Her name is Professor Margaret Murray of University College, London and her published works say a lot about her interests and beliefs. They include *The Witch-Cult In Western Europe* and *The God Of The Witches*. None enjoy long-lasting academic credibility.

Professor Murray is interested by three facets of the case. The fact that the body is discovered lodged in a tree, that its right hand is reportedly missing and that its name is a diminutive of Belladonna.

If a woman is believed to be a witch, she argues, then burial in a tree makes sense because the tree supposedly imprisons the spirit, which cannot then roam and cause further harm; and of course, in Arthurian legend, Merlin was sealed inside a tree to imprison him.

The professor says severing a hand is a mark of a black magic execution and cites a macabre belief in the magical powers attributable to it. She refers to the so-called 'Hand of Glory', chopped in the dead of night from the still warm corpse of a hanged malefactor. Dried or cured or preserved in candle grease such a severed hand supposedly has the power to protect its new owner from evil spirits or to reveal the whereabouts of hidden treasure.

Professor Murray is also interested in the history of the supernatural in the locality. The nearest pub to the site of the Wych-Elm, *The Gypsies Tent*, has a history of reported hauntings going back to the English Civil War and is said to be associated with witch's sabbats in the Hagley Woods over the centuries. Margaret Murray wants the Chief Constable to focus efforts on finding and questioning members of local witches' covens.

The Gypsies Tent Pub

It doesn't help rational consideration of the murder much when on the 14th of February 1945 a second bizarre, local killing occurs. This time it's an elderly farm worker, a 74-year-old, Charles Walton of

Lower Quinton. He's found pinned to the ground by a pitchfork and with a trouncing hook buried in his neck. A large cross has been carved into his chest. For a time, at Professor Murray's urging, the police treat the two cases as connected. That murder too remains unsolved.

Growing up in rural England in the second half of the twentieth century sometimes feels much like living in a purportedly rational country in which you only have to scratch the surface to find belief in the occult, and pitchfork murders definitely feature. In the days before regular access to newspapers and television news and the internet, the grapevine in the West Country of England carried a slew of stories, real or imaginary, of ritual murder, usually in the Cotswolds, that supposed haven of macabre beliefs and sacrificial fertility offerings. In such a febrile atmosphere, Charles Walton's slaughter is seized on by Professor Murray as further evidence that satanic forces are at work in Worcestershire. Among some locals the belief is temporarily founded that the secret of Bella's death rests with a mysterious coven which will do anything necessary to safeguard itself. In time such theories fade in popularity. After all the hand wasn't missing from the scene at all. And if witches have ever flourished in the area, they've left precious little evidence of their passing behind them.

There's another problem with the Hand of Glory theory. There is no severed hand only some missing finger bones. Several other bones are missing too and although most are subsequently recovered some of the leg bones aren't found at all.

Local clergy and churchgoers react to the talk of witchcraft and black magic with the less than charitable suggestion that Bella may have been a gypsy, a Romany woman, whose grievous offence led to her ritual death at the hands of her own kin. There's not a shred of evidence for this beyond the fact that gypsies have traditionally encamped for short periods in fields near the crime scene. As a consequence, the police concentrate some of their search for missing persons on travelling families known to visit the area. Inquiries after a number of gypsies, many of them part of the massive group among the English whose surname is Smith, do a great deal more to divert police time unproductively.

For the record, Bella was not wearing any clothing or item of Romany origin at the time of her death. And whilst there have been examples of gypsy punishment by kinfolk banishment, as far as records show, ritual murder or even straightforward execution by family members has never occurred.

A SEXUAL MOTIVE

Among other lines of inquiry, the police wonder if Bella might be a prostitute driven to meet her death in the woods but deem it unlikely given that her age is probably mid to late-thirties. It may be less likely that an older woman would be making her living from prostitution but in wartime who knows? The fact which negates this theory is the lack of any reports of missing prostitutes matching Bella's physical description around the conurbation and the fact that her remains appear to be still clad in slip, corset and knickers.

An alternate theory is that Bella might have been among those leaving the nearby cities at night to camp in laybys along the roads so as to escape the constant air-raids. If so she might have been unfortunate enough to fall in with a rapist and murderer but again this is rendered unlikely as in death she's still wearing the remains of her underwear and there's no relevant missing person report in the files.

The final speculation is that Bella may have been murdered by a lover aggrieved at her becoming pregnant. The pregnancy element is refuted by the autopsy work of Professor Webster and since the police couldn't find out who Bella was, they thought it futile to try to find a husband or lover who might have killed her, especially if she was killed in the woods and hidden straight away as Professor Webster believed.

FOREIGNER OR SPY

The reasons for the police asking if Bella might be a spy or connected to a spy ring is the absence of a credible English missing person. Could Bella therefore be an alien, living in the West Midlands unregistered and thus here illegally or criminally?

In the early 1940s the region is awash with crucial munitions and steel plants. Birmingham, Coventry and Wolverhampton are being bombed nightly by the Luftwaffe and secret command bunkers exist such as that situated in the Drakelow Tunnels near Kidderminster. Furthermore, two Jewish, German emigres are engaged in highly secret atomic bomb research at Birmingham University and their work is about to be handed over to the Americans on Churchill's orders to inform Oppenheimer's Manhattan Project. There's plenty of valuable military information which the Germans would want to get hold of and the newspapers are rich with warnings for the public to beware of Nazi spies, male or female.

Periodically there are rumours of German parachutists landing in the vicinity of Hagley and the Home Guard regularly conduct extensive searches of Hagley Woods and the Clent Hills.

Successful espionage depends upon creating a cover identity in a community allowing someone to move reasonably freely. Language skills are a must and the spy can carry nothing which might give away their true loyalties. This includes removing labels from clothing to disguise its origins. The lack of surviving labels in Bella's clothing and the possibility that her recent dentistry is continental can be viewed as circumstantial proof that she might have been a spy.
One of the more ludicrous theories aired at the time is that Bella came down by parachute and died because she landed in the tree, a near impossibility in reality considering the narrowness of the access into the hollow tree. It's argued that locals finding a body

wedged in a tree amid a sea of collapsed parachute silk might choose to steal the valuable fabric rather than report it but it defies logic that there would be no other sign she'd come from an aeroplane, such as the parachute harness she'd have to have worn and it seems unlikely that Bella would jump in nothing warmer or offering better protection than a skirt and cardigan.

Alternatively, if as a spy who'd parachuted down in the vicinity, Bella had landed safely and divested herself of her flying gear, the civil and military authorities (even the members of any of Churchill's Special Units) would have wanted her taken alive for the information in her head. Who would have killed her near to the drop zone and hidden the body in a tree? It's scarcely credible as possibilities go.

The theory that Bella was involved in espionage doesn't ever go away completely and in 1968, the writer Donald McCormick claims to have seen previously unrevealed wartime papers from German military intelligence, the Abwehr, relating to a female spy code-named Clara or Clarabella who was allegedly dropped into the West Midlands in 1941 but never subsequently made radio contact with her handlers in Berlin.

McCormick refers to interviews with an ex-Nazi called Franz Rathgeb, based in the Midlands during the war years. Rathgeb talks in turn of a fellow agent, Lehrer, with a Dutch girlfriend from Utrecht who lived in Birmingham. Her name is something like Clarabella Dronkers. She is small, has irregular teeth, and is supposedly a German spy who had visited England before the war. Indeed, Rathgelb tells McCormick that she had a specific connection with a Stourbridge man with whom she'd been in an unhappy relationship. Rathgelb states that he last saw Clara in 1941.

The trouble is that the only verifiable fact is that a Dutch national named Johannes Marinus Dronkers was executed as a spy in

December 1942. There's nothing in the records about a Clarabella Dronkers and we're pushed back for confirmation to third party evidence from a woman called Una Mossop about the 'Dutch piece' who hung around with a spy named Van Ralt and his friend Jack, the munitions worker who liked to pose as a British officer, to whom we'll turn next.

JACK MOSSOP AND VAN RALT

The next proffered solution to the Bella mystery is founded upon the more prosaic motivation for murder of a lovers' quarrel. In 1953 a woman contacts the Wolverhampton Express and Star. She gives her name as Anna of Claverley and claims to know who killed Bella. The woman is unmasked as one Una Mossop, living near Kenilworth in Warwickshire. Una has several sessions with the police and although these are held in secret, an Express and Star reporter, Wilford Byford-Jones, under the by-line *Quaestor*, writes several columns about Anna and the case, using information drawn from Una's confessions.

At the outbreak of the war, Una's husband, Jack, is working in an aircraft factory in Birmingham, a reserved occupation so he isn't subsequently called up into the army. He doesn't earn much so it surprises Una in 1940 when he seems to come into money. He buys expensive clothes she can't see how he can afford and an officer's uniform he's not entitled to wear. Una thinks the money comes from a new friend he's made; a Dutchman called Van Ralt. He's also drinking too much and Una can't cope with it and throws him out.

Late in 1941 Jack Mossop returns to Una in a terrible state, suffering nightmares about a murder. Coaxed by Una, he tells her all about it. He went for a drive and ended up drinking with his friend, Van Ralt and *his Dutch piece* in The Lyttleton Arms in Clent, near Hagley. Van Ralt and the woman were rowing. At Van Ralt's suggestion, Jack took them for a ride in Van Ralt's car up Hagley Hill, with the woman in the passenger seat and Van Ralt in the back. The row escalated and Van Ralt attacked the woman, who slumped forward, presumably strangled. Jack pulled the car off the road and then helped Van Ralt carry the body some 25 yards and squeeze it into a hollow tree trunk. Jack and Van Ralt never meet again.

There's no way to verify Una Mossop's story because her husband is admitted to a mental hospital in Stafford in 1942 and dies there soon afterwards.

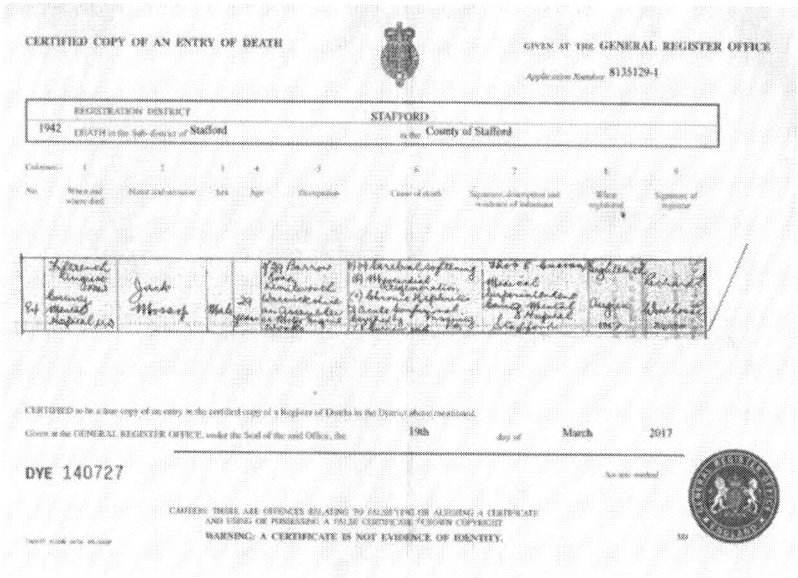
CERTIFIED COPY OF AN ENTRY OF DEATH

GIVEN AT THE GENERAL REGISTER OFFICE

Application Number 8135129-1

REGISTRATION DISTRICT STAFFORD

1942 DEATH in the Sub-district of Stafford in the County of Stafford

No.	When and where died	Name and surname	Sex	Age	Occupation	Cause of death	Signature, description and residence of informant	When registered	Signature of registrar
84	[illegible]	Jack Mossop	Male	[illegible]	[illegible]	[illegible]	[illegible] Stafford	[illegible] 1942	[illegible]

CERTIFIED to be a true copy of an entry in the certified copy of a Register of Deaths in the District above mentioned.

Given at the GENERAL REGISTER OFFICE, under the Seal of the said Office, the 19th day of March 2017

DYE 140727

CAUTION: THERE ARE OFFENCES RELATING TO FALSIFYING OR ALTERING A CERTIFICATE AND USING OR POSSESSING A FALSE CERTIFICATE ©CROWN COPYRIGHT

WARNING: A CERTIFICATE IS NOT EVIDENCE OF IDENTITY.

What we do have on police files is the incident of the parked car containing the RAF officer and the sleeping woman on the backseat.

The other part of Una's story ties the purported murder back to espionage. It's that Van Ralt had drawn Jack Mossop into securing munitions information for the Germans and that *Bella* knew too much about the spy-ring and was endangering it. However, Jack Mossop never told Una the woman's name.

AN AGENT CODE-NAMED CLARA

The link between Bella's fate and wartime espionage is resurrected again in the story of Clara Bauerle.

Declassified wartime material from the National Archives includes a file for a Czech national named Josef Jakobs (1898-1941). His history covers his detention by the Home Guard in Cambridgeshire after a parachute landing in Ramsey on the 31st of January 1941. Jakobs is interrogated and on the 15th of August 1941 becomes the last man to be executed at The Tower of London. He's shot by firing squad as a Nazi agent.

Jakob's file contains a picture postcard he's carrying in his pocket when caught. The card bears a photograph of a woman he claims as his lover. He gives her name as Clara Bauerle. The back of the card carries a dedication. It reads *My Dear. I love you for ever. Your Clara. Landau July 1940.*

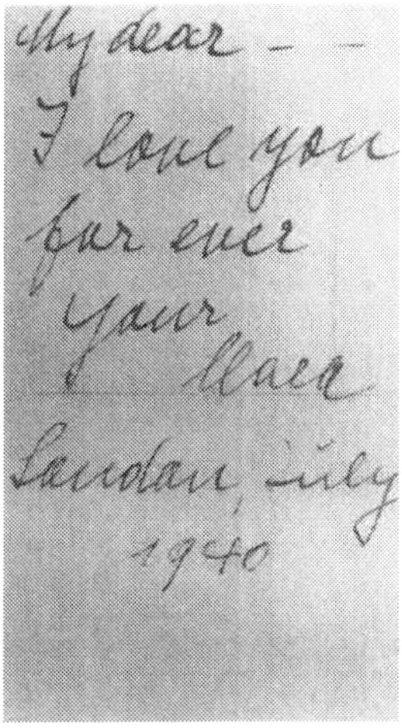

This Clara is a cabaret singer and sometime movie actress. MI5 check their records and sources and she exists all right. Born Klare Sophie Bauerle in Ulm near Stuttgart on the 29th of June 1906 which means that in 1941 she was 35 years old. Her career included the better part of two years working the music halls of the West Midlands from her arrival on the 20th October 1930 until her departure from Warwick as recorded in the Central Register of

Aliens on the 21st of June 1932. She spoke English with a Brummie accent and English audiences sometimes call her Clarabella.

Jakobs recounts how he first meets Clara in Hamburg singing with the Bernhard Ette Orchestra at the Cafe Dreyer. She's the former lover of a U-Boat medical officer, well-connected in the Nazi party, with possible links to Goering and has been recruited as a secret agent with the code-name Clara. However, Jakobs says plans to parachute her into the vicinity of Birmingham will now be aborted, because he has not established radio contact proving it's safe to send her. Of course, Jakobs doesn't want his captors to go looking for Clara and even though apparently truthful about the rest of it, he may have been lying on this point or her handlers choose to send her in anyway. The odd thing is that Jakobs appears convinced that his Clara has never been to England but perhaps that's another lie hidden among the truths. Surely her fluency, regional accent and geographical knowledge are the very skills which best fit her to spy on the factories and anti-aircraft defences of the city of Birmingham.

There is said to be no trace of Clara Bauerle back in Germany after the early months of 1941; no subsequent concerts or gramophone recordings or movie appearances carrying her name; signalling a sudden end to her well-established show business career. This means Clara Bauerle makes a potentially plausible candidate for the unidentified body in the Wych-Elm in Hagley Woods or so Alison Vale states as a strong possibility in her article for the Independent on the 22nd of March 2013.

Unfortunately, the Independent should have checked its facts before going to print. If they had they might have found the holes in their evidence and realised that Clara Bauerle could not be Bella.

Firstly, our Bella is only five feet in height. Clara is described by Karel Richter, another captured German spy who knew both Jakobs and Clara, as tall, nearly six feet in height. Secondly Clara did not have buckled front teeth. Thirdly it isn't true that Clara's recording career stopped early in 1941. She was still recording throughout that year and 1942. Fourthly she died in Berlin not in England, on the 16th December 1942.

Clara Bauerle was not dropped by parachute into England in the first few months of 1941 and she certainly didn't end up incarcerated in a hollow tree.

A VERY COLD CASE

So, is the woman found in the hollow tree the Bella in the pub remembered by Warwick Plant; the singer and pianist to whom his mother donated a pair of shoes? If so did she fall foul of Van Ralt or Franz Rathgelb? Did she imperil some lucrative scam taking money from Berlin or the very existence of a spy network reporting other than to Clara's own Abwehr masters? Is she the same woman some identified as Clarabella Dronkers or Una Mossop described as the *Dutch piece*? Was Bella a spy or a foreigner? The absence of labels in her clothing and the failure to establish a British identity for her corpse make it a possibility that she came from overseas but whether she was a spy or the poor woman without means of support who played piano at the pub for a few coins, nobody can say.

Hampering all attempts to investigate Bella's case today is the cavalier manner in which the evidence has been handled over the years or the deliberate destruction of the files. Police notes, witness statements, original photograph negatives from the crime scene, archive material and even the Coroner's Report to the 1943 inquest are all gone. Astoundingly Bella's remains are also missing so DNA profiling is out of the question.

Bella wasn't buried in any local cemetery at the time because her bones were taken for examination by Professor Webster. He in turn left them to his successor, Doctor Griffiths at the Birmingham University Medical School from where they have somehow disappeared, allegedly following office moves. Is it possible that someone authorised their burial? If they did there should be a record of the fact but there isn't one to be found. Who knows where those bones are now? Without them there's nothing on which to conduct modern testing to trace Bella's descendants and find her identity.

However, for those who prefer conspiracy theories and would wish to claim the murder is related to Nazi spying activities and to attribute it to the intelligence services or one of Churchill's Special Units, then you may care to know one other probably irrelevant fact. Around the time that the Bella papers disappeared from the Worcestershire Records Office, a young woman is starting her first employment there, a newly-qualified archivist called Stella Whitehouse and her boyfriend works for MI5. Stella marries him, taking his surname and going on to enjoy a spectacular career in the security services, rising to the dizzy heights of Director General of MI5 under her married name – Stella Rimington.

Trying to look at such a 'cold case' calmly after a hiatus approaching eighty years, it still might be that the true story of Bella in the Wych-Elm is that of a woman murdered in a lover's quarrel. Perhaps, knowing the woods well, the killer took her there deliberately and hid her body in a tree he'd already earmarked for the purpose. As for the supposedly severed hand, the missing bones are probably simply the work of foxes who bury edible things to retrieve when times are leaner.

The hollow tree is long gone. Almost irretrievably damaged by Jack Pound's axe as the police extracted the skeleton, the tree eventually died. Even here misinformation prevails. John Stalker made a television programme about Bella, filming in the wrong location, on Wychbury Hill. Many people now believe that was the actual tree. You won't find it there anymore though; it was eventually burnt down to a mere stump. Whether it was hit by lightning or the subject of arson, is a matter of speculation.

But the mystery of Bella...the mystery continues.

BELLA'S LEGACY

Until 2005, Bella had a case file with West Mercia Police as an unsolved murder. As with the passage of time the perpetrators and potential adult witnesses must by now be deceased, the case file was closed and a copy of the closing report is included at the back of this book.

An article by the journalist Richard Askwith in the Independent newspaper on 18th August 1999 inspired composer Simon Holt to create a chamber opera unsurprisingly called *Who Put Bella In The Witch-Elm*. The opera is set amid supernatural occurrences at the pub as the ghost of Bella appears to tell her fate. In so setting his opera, Holt acknowledges the long-standing tradition in *The Gypsies Tent*, now re-named *The Badger's Sett*, of attributing all unexplained phenomena to the ghost the staff and customers have always referred to as Bella. The opera premiered at Aldebrough to some acclaim in 2003. Soon after, for its own 75th anniversary celebrations, the Stourbridge Theatre Company commissioned a play from David Morris about the murder and a Coventry band, The Pristines, named an album *Who Put Bella In The Witch-Elm*.

However, Bella's longest-lasting legacy may yet prove to be the sporadic reports of ghostly sightings in Hagley Woods, along that stretch of the A456 or the pub once known as *The Gypsies Tent*. Or perhaps it'll be the sporadic outbursts of graffiti: *Who put Bella In The Witch-Elm*, like the slogan which still disfigures the stone base of Lord Cobham's obelisk on the crest of Wychbury Hill.

OUTSTANDING QUESTIONS

In conclusion and with the benefit of hindsight and modern investigative thinking, here are the questions to which I'd like answers:

Where are Bella's remains? Were they interred after Professor Webster retired or if misplaced, who by and when?

Where exactly in Hagley Wood was the hollow tree?

Why did graffiti on walls seek to identify the body as Luebella or Bella? Was Bella or some-such actually her name?

Were the shoes found near the tree actually Bella's?

Why was the story of a Bella playing and singing for coins in local pubs not followed up and documented?

What was the provenance of the clothes Bella was wearing? Were they English or continental? Was the lack of labels a sinister clue or were the clothes bought as unlabelled seconds at a market?

Was Bella's dental work English or continental and how thorough in wartime was the search of dental records or had she seen an unregistered dentist who was never therefore asked to check her records? And where is all the evidence of responses to this and other enquiries in the police case files?

Who was Van Ralt or Raalt? Who was his alleged Dutch girlfriend? Were either of them spying for the Germans and if so on what targets – the work of the munitions factories, the efficacy of the Luftwaffe's bombing of the region or on the research into nuclear weapons being conducted at Birmingham University?

Why are there so many missing elements in the police files? Where are the reports which were apparently passed in the 1950s to the Worcestershire County Records Office from where they subsequently disappeared?

Where is the Coroner's Report of 1943?

What would be the logical motive for killing Bella?

Why was Bella's body concealed in a hollow tree rather than being buried? Doesn't this point to local knowledge of the woods by the perpetrator or even advance planning?

Is the Jack Mossop story plausible and can any supporting evidence be found?

Where are the remains of the hollow tree so badly damaged by Jack Pound's axe?

And finally, the mystery itself that it would almost be a shame to solve here and now: who was Bella and who put her in the Wych-Elm?

FURTHER READING

Donald McCORMICK: Murder By Witchcraft (Arrow Books 1969)

Joyce COLEY: *Bella - An Unsolved Murder* (History Into Present 2007)

Anne BRADFORD: *Foul Deeds & Suspicious Deaths Around Worcester* (Wharnecliffe Books 2008)

Paul NEWMAN: *Under the Shadow of Meon Hill: The Lower Quinton & Hagley Wood Murders* (Abraxas 2011)

Alex MERRILL: *Who Put Bella In The Wych Elm - Vol. 1 The Crime Scene Revisited* (APS Books 2018)

DOCUMENTATION

1.FORENSIC REPORT 1943

WEST MIDLAND FORENSIC SCIENCE LABORATORY,
NEWTON STREET, BIRMINGHAM, 4,
23rd April, 1943

DIRECTOR
James M. Webster, M.A., B.Sc., MBChB., F.R.C.S.

HUMAN REMAINS FOUND IN A HOLLOW TREE IN HAGLEY WOOD ON THE MAIN BIRMINGHAM-KIDDERMINSTER ROAD

On the 20th April, 1943, at about 6.30pm, in company with Officers of the Worcestershire County Police Force, and with other assistance I recovered from the hollow bole of the stump of an elm tree in Hagley Wood on the main Birmingham-Kidderminster Road certain human remains and garments. These remains consisted of a disarticulated skeleton. The skeleton was incomplete and at the time I recovered a human tibia or shin bone about 12 yards from this tree. On the 22nd instant I received from the Worcestershire Constabulary a left pelvic bone, a right femur, and a right fibula. The combined bones make up a human skeleton, and they are parts of one body and one body only. The skeleton is incomplete and is minus the right tibia or shin bone, part of the hyoid bone, a patella, and some of the small bones of the hands and feet.

Skull

The skull was in two parts, consisting of the head, which lay exposed on the floor of the tree bole, and the lower jaw, which was in line with the disarticulated vertebrae under the overhanging entrance to the hollow bole. This skull is undoubtedly human and is that of a female.

Upper Jaw

In the upper jaw the two central incisors, the left lateral incisor, and the second right molar are missing. From examination of the sockets, however, these had dropped out post-mortem and were present in the head at the time of this woman's death. The teeth which remain are in good condition except that the second left premolar is carious. There is no evidence of this person having suffered from pyorrhoea. Neither of the third molars in the upper jaw has erupted. The teeth, moreover, are clean.

There are no marks of injury on the skull, and all the soft tissue has gone. A few hairs were still adherent to the top of the skull. The inside of the skull shows a considerable quantity of old blood on the right side. This, however, is so decomposed that it is impossible to say if this blood was shed ante- mortem or was due to post-mortem postural changes. It is true that this old blood is situated over the right middle meningeal artery, but, in the absence of any injury to the skull, it is reasonable to suppose that this did not come from the middle meningeal artery during life. The sutures of the skull are plainly marked on the outside, and on the inside, they are still plainly visible. These markings disappear in late middle life. The sagittal suture shows commencing obliteration when viewed from the inside and this condition usually commences at the age of 25 years and closure may be quite marked at the age of 40 years. Hence, from the condition of the sutures the age of this skull is quite definitely between 25 and 40 years.

There is a slight anomaly with regard to the dentition in the upper jaw in that the third molars, which are un-erupted in this case, usually erupt in females at the age of between 18 and 24 years, but the eruption of third molars is notoriously irregular. Hence, no reliance as to age can be placed upon the teeth, and they are infinitely less important from the point of view of age than the sutures.

There is a little bloodstaining all over this skull on the outside.

Lower Jaw

In the lower jaw the dentition has been complete, the third molars having erupted. The teeth are in fairly good condition, but the first left molar is extremely carious, and the first right molar had been extracted a considerable time before death, since the socket had had time to heal completely. There is nothing particularly distinctive about the teeth except for the fact that there is slight overlapping of the incisors. The best way, I consider of describing the incisor teeth is that there would have been a noticeable irregularity of the incisors. Further, with regard to the lower jaw, this, when found by me, was in line with the spine.

Tightly pressed over the lower jaw in the cavity of the mouth I found part of the khaki or mustard coloured dress which the deceased was wearing at the time of death. So far as this thrust over the teeth margin and so firmly adherent to the teeth was this part of the apparel that I do not consider it likely – I cannot say impossible – that this came into the mouth prior to death, and, if so this would have been capable of causing death from asphyxia.

Clavicles

The two clavicles are present, and these show no sign of disease or injury, recent or old.

Hyoid Bone

I recovered from the debris below the lower jaw a small piece of thin fragile bone which in my opinion constitutes one of the cornua of a human hyoid bone. The rest of the hyoid was missing and this might very well be accounted for by the ravages of animals. It is obvious from this portion of the hyoid that ossification had not taken place between the body of the hyoid and the cornua – a condition which again places this woman under the age of 40.

Scapulae

Both scapulae are present, but neither of these bones shows any distinctive feature.

Sternum

The sternum is present except the xiphi sternum, and there is incomplete fusion between the manubrium and the body of the sternum. Whilst it is true that the union of the xiphoid to the body usually takes place at about 40 years of age, and the union of the manubrium and the body at a much later period, the ossification of this bone is again notoriously irregular, and, though it would appear from the condition of the manubrium and body, that this woman was over 40, the fact that the xiphoid and the body have not united outweighs the former evidence with regard to this bone, and in my opinion, so far as the sternum is concerned the balance of evidence is that again this woman was under 40.

Humeri

The two humeri are present and measure in the longest diameter 28.2cm. Here again there is no distinctive feature, the bones showing neither injury nor disease. All the epiphyses have joined up.

Radii and Ulnae

The bones of the forearm, namely, the radius and ulna, are present on both sides the radii measuring 19cm. Again there is no distinctive feature. All the epiphyses have joined up.

Spine and Ribs

The complete spine and ribs are present. None of these shows injury or ante-mortem abnormality. Further, there are none of the changes due to age on the spine, and there is no lipping or evidence of arthritis. The curvatures of the spine are normal.

Pelvis

The pelvis is in three parts, namely, the sacrum, and the two separate hip or iliac bones. The sex characteristics of the pelvis are unquestionably female. Both pelvic bones have suffered considerably from the ravages of animals, and small parts of them are missing. There is one feature in the two hip bones, namely, the well-marked condition of the pre-auricular sulcus, which is frequently associated with previous childbirth, but this is not conclusive. The epiphysis between the crest of the ilium and the rest of the bone is firmly united - a process which takes place by the end of the 25th year.

Femora

The two femora are present and measure 4.1cm. in length. The epiphyses have united at both the upper and lower ends - a condition usually completed by about the 22nd year. The trabeculae of bone at the lower end of the femur are not quite continuous across the line of the epiphysis, again showing that this person had not reached advanced age. These bones again show no distinctive feature.

Fibulae and Tibiae

Both fibulae are present and again show no distinctive features, the epiphyses being united. The right tibia is missing, but the left tibia, which was found at some distance from the tree, is present, though incomplete, the maleolus having been chewed away. The estimated longest measurement of this bone is 30cm.

Foot Bones

Most of the small bones of the feet are present. There is nothing distinctive about these, and examination of the two first metatarsals gives no indication that this woman had suffered from any distinctive deformity such as bunions - a conclusion which is borne out by an examination of her shoes.

CONCLUSIONS

The following are my conclusions with regard to the skeleton.

Sex

There can be no doubt that this is a female skeleton. The female characteristics are so evident in the pelvis and skull as to leave one in no dubiety about this.

Age

One can be quite certain that this woman was over 25 years of age and under 40. From the condition of the sutures of the skull, this woman was in my opinion someyears under 40, and I would put her probable approximate age as 35, that is to say 35 either plus or minus a few years.

Stature

Using Karl Pearson's formulae, I .am of opinion that this was a woman definitely under average height, and my estimates with these formulae place her at about 60 inches in height.

Accident, Suicide, or Murder

There is no indication in the skeleton or in the clothing as to which of these conditions played a part in this woman's death. Consideration, however, of the

bole of the tree in which this skeleton was found leads me to the conclusion that this was much more likely to be murder than the other two propositions. The entrance to this tree was extremely narrow arid would have caused not merely inconvenience, but actual injury if even small woman of this nature should have forced herself into the tree. Further, I do not think that this was

a likely position for committing suicide. Accident can, I think, be entirely ruled out. The tree, however, afforded an excellent concealment for a murder. From the position of the skeleton in the bole of the tree, I am of opinion that this woman was pushed in feet first. Moreover, she could only have been pushed in conveniently either before rigor mortis set in or after rigor mortis had passed off. If the body had been kept until rigor mortis had passed off, putrefaction would have commenced, and it is extremely unlikely that the murderer would have kept the body until it had got into this condition. Hence I am of opinion that this body was pushed into the tree before rigor mortis had set in. This being so, it is likely that the murder was committed in near vicinity to the tree, or, if committed at a distance, the murderer must have had a conveyance to enable him to get the body to the tree before rigor mortis set in.

Time of Death

With regard to the time of death, I must point out that once bones become completely stripped of the flesh, they may remain in a dried condition similar to that we found in this case, for years. Hence it is only possible to give a minimum time for a body to have lain where it was found. The flesh has completely gone from these bones, but, although the sutures of the skull are not closed, they have not fallen apart. Moreover, I found that there was considerable growth of the roots of this tree through the remainder of the clothing, and, taking into consideration all these factors, I am of opinion that this body must have been there a minimum period of 18 months, but may have been there for a very considerably longer period.

Shoes

It would appear probable that the pair of shoes recovered, one from the bole of the tree, and the other at same distance are connected with this body. These shoes are black shoes, size 5½, and from the information which I obtained, are probably made by the Waterfoot Company, Lancashire. Inspector Williams, however, following his visit to Northampton, has considerably more information with regard to these shoes, and this seems to me a likely line to follow up.

Description of the Deceased

Combining my own and Dr Lund's observations, it appears to me that a very likely description of the deceased would be:

A woman aged be 25 and 40 years, most probably around about 35 years of age, 5ft. in height, with light (mousy) brown hair; no undue prominence of the teeth but Noticeable irregularity of the front teeth in the lower jaw; clad in a dark blue and light khaki or mustard coloured woollen cardigan with cloth covered buttons and a belt of a slightly brighter shade of blue than the blue stripes in the cardigan itself. A light khaki or mustard coloured woollen cloth skirt with a side zip fastener, a peach-coloured taffeta rayon underskirt, navy blue interlock cotton knickers, corsets and black crepe-soled shoes. The above person has been missing for at least 18 months. She was wearing a rolled gold enamelled ring.

James Webster

Professor of Forensic Medicine and Toxicology, University of Birmingham

2. WEST MERCIA POLICE CASE CLOSURE REPORT

NOTE

The document reproduced below has been reproduced in full, without change, except for the correction of obvious misspellings and the use of capital letters for headings to make the report easier to read.

REGARDING

ALLEGED MURDER AT HAGLEY WOOD DECEASED UNKNOWN

19th APRIL 1943

Commissioned by: Detective Chief Superintendent T. Albutt

Author: Detective Chief Inspector I Nicholls

Report Date: 13 July 2005

INTRODUCTION

The purpose of this document is to record the review of the above file which pertains to the investigation surrounding the recovery of the remains of a female from within the naturally hollowed-out trunk of an elm tree located within Hagley Wood adjacent to the main Birmingham to Kidderminster Road. This road is now designated as this A456. The remains were first reported on 19 April 1943. It was estimated that the body had been so located for a period of not less than eighteen months.

When recovered the skeleton was disarticulated and certain bones were missing. The nature of the bones missing would induce a presumption that the absence was as a result of wildlife intervention rather than being removed at the time of or immediately after death. It was assessed that the individual has entered the cavity feet first, and the probability of this occurring willingly or intentionally was remote thus it was determined that this matter was an offence of murder. It is, I contend, most certainty an unexplained death however in the absence of a specific cause of death or indeed any identified injuries which indicate the individual was subjected to trauma, that to make the leap to a murder is questionable. However, in line with the current standards contained within the National Crime Recording Standards (Revised April 2004) specifically the 'Balance of Probability' test, the balance is that the individual was subjected to unlawful actions, which lead directly or indirectly to her death

EXECUTIVE SUMMARY

Incident occurred at the height of Axis bombing of the West Midlands conurbation.

The deceased has yet to be identified

Investigation centred on the identification of the deceased.

Final resting-place still unknown.

Investigation skewed by false reports.

No further witnesses identified.

Forensic opportunities examined however no advantages identified.

Two potential suspects were identified as a result of information in 1953, one of whom was dead, the other remains untraced.

INVESTIGATION

The investigation of the offence centred primarily on the identification of the deceased, and through that process identifying any person who may have been involved in the death. The identification phase centred upon the shoes retrieved from the scene, circulations appertaining to the deceased, and examination of missing persons allegedly missing.

To contextualise the event occurred at a time when considerable bombing by Axis forces was occurring within the Birmingham/Wolverhampton/Coventry conurbation, and thus it was considerably more common for persons to be transient and obviously death without record was a more frequent occurrence.

During the course of the investigation a number of factors caused a skewing of the resources involved.

The first issue, which took up considerable effort, was the series of chalked messages upon walls throughout the West Midlands conurbation from Wolverhampton, into the Black Country and also into the city centre of Birmingham. The chalking's were undertaken over a protracted period of time. The reason for and also the author(s) of the chalking's were not established despite considerable investment.

Additionally considerable effort was expended attempting to identify the whereabouts of a Mary Wenman/Lee/Beaver, a traveller who at one time resided close to the location where the cadaver was recovered A soldier HEYWOOD, who was formerly having a relationship with the woman and sought to re-establish the relationship, initiated this. By a number of guises he used the Police to initiate an investigation to ascertain her whereabouts. The reality of the situation came to light and HEYWOOD subsequently admitted the details.

Bella TONKS was raised as a possibility following a media circulation. The name 'Bella' was seemingly derived from the chalk writings on the walls throughout the West Midlands conurbation and as such the link to the enquiry was questionable. That said, the individual Bella Tonks was identified as living under her maiden name in Heath Hays.

Ann FORREST a traveller, was identified as having lived close to the deposition site, and was raised as potentially the deceased as a result of this. Enquiries traced FORREST in April 1944 as being alive and well.

Bella BEECH was draw to the inquiry's attention following her disappearance from bombed premises in West Ealing London. She had left the bombed premises to live in the Birmingham area, and contact had ceased. Enquiries traced this woman to a hospital in the London area where she was working as a nurse.

Bella LUER was a woman who moved from London to undertake factory work. The contact chain with persons in London was broken and thus she was raised as a possibility as being the deceased. Again the major factor was the term 'Bella'. Enquiries traced a Bella Luer as being a resident al Goring On Thames, however this individual was not definitely linked to the Bella Luer who was formerly resident in the Stamford Hill area of London.

Violet GOODE was a female who had been involved in a relationship with Thomas Henry Truman resulting in his relationship with his wife Gladys Truman failing. Subsequently Truman returned to his wife and a spurious assertion was made that GOODE had been killed to make way for this return. GOODE was identified as being alive and well, working and living in Stourbridge.

LINES OF ENQUIRY NOT FINALISED

Dinah CURLEY aka O'GRADY

This line of enquiry commenced with the report of the above named person being missing by a woman, the recorded details of whom were Mrs M Lavin 56 Stanley Street, Manchester. This report prompted enquiries to trace both CURLEY and the reporter LAVIN. The thrust of the latter was following a labourer called Jack (John Edward) Lavin.

Document 112 outlines page two of details of a number of persons reported missing for the time appropriate to the believed death, provides a number of persons albeit there is no reference to investigation into the circumstances of their disappearance.

From the information supplied there is insufficient to identify whether CURLEY aka O'Grady in fact existed.

Enquiries to trace the person M LAVIN failed to do so however there were a number of coincidences with the labourer Jack LAVIN. His wife was Mrs Mary LAVIN nee DOWLING. Their home was 40 Lawrence Street, Stockport, Manchester. The reporter of the missing person allegedly resided at 56 Stanley Street, Cheetham, Manchester however she moved in about 1941 to an address in 32 Robert Street, Cheetham Manchester with a family called Lynch.

The LYNCH family subsequently removed to an address in Haverfordwest. Jack Lavin was employed on a contract in the St. David's area of west Wales, residing at an address on the Fishguard to Haverfordwest Road. Whilst there he was joined by his wife Mary.

Enquiries in the Haverfordwest area for the reporter LAVIN identified an address of 73 Belle Vue Terrace Haverfordwest until 30 March 1943 from where she removed to an address of 9 Claremont, Ripon, Yorkshire.

The LYNCH family removed six months earlier to an address in Kettering, Northamptonshire

Jack LAVIN was sought for non-payment at fines in Northamptonshire. In respect of Ripon, to where Mrs M Lavin allegedly moved following leaving Haverfordwest. Coincidentally a Mr John Edward LAVIN resided at 9, Claremont, Ripon from 9 March 1943. The latter's previous address was recorded as being 40 Lawrence Street, Stockport.

Thus with all the co-incidences it is highly probable that the reporter for the missing person was Mrs Mary LAVIN, the wife of Jack (John Edward) LAVIN, despite denials by him of any knowledge and links to the 56 Stanley Street address. There is nothing on the file to indicate that Mary LAVIN was interviewed and challenged about these issues. The reasons for the denial and the report being made remain unclear, however it is probable that it was personal gain, and that the alleged missing person CURLEY aka O'Grady was a fictitious individual.

There are on file a number of communications which, it would seem prudent not to follow as the basis for the content is at best questionable.

SUSPECTS

During 1953, his former wife, UNA HAINSWORTH, identified JACK MOSSOP as a potential suspect following a submission. MOSSOP, in later life was suffering from mental illness and died in a mental institution in 1942. In 1932 the relationship of MOSSOP and the now HAINSWORTH produced a son, Julian MOSSOP, who remained with his mother until 1949, when he went to London and there became involved in criminality. At the time of the discovery of the deceased, Julian MOSSOP was eleven years of age, living in Kenilworth and as such can be discounted as a suspect. Mrs HAINSWORTH seemingly had some history, as it would appear that the removal from the Kenilworth address left behind considerable debts.

Following their divorce and in the later part of his life Hainsworth and Mossop met where he alleged he was losing his mind, suffering from mental images of a woman in a tree leering at him. At this stage Hainsworth was obviously not aware of the Hagley body as it was yet to be discovered, and thought it was a delaying tactic for resolving issues. With the discovery of the body and subsequent media attention in a pictorial, Hainsworth wrote a letter signing it 'Anna'. At that stage some assertions with regard to witchcraft had been made and she wished not to be associated with it.

The story she outlined was that a Dutch male called Van Ralt (term also includes the spelling Van Raalt hereafter) came to her home in 1940. He was seemingly without regular employment albeit he had considerable funds. Hainsworth made an aside that Van Ralt may have been a spy. This aside seems to be the basis for later conjecture that the death involved spies.

In March or April 1941, MOSSOP arrived home noticeably having had drank alcohol, and in an agitated state when he allegedly stated that he had been to the Lyttleton Arms with Van RALT and the 'Dutch piece' (Presumably this meant a female either Dutch in nationality or associated with the Dutchman Van RALT). MOSSOP allegedly stated that the female had become awkward then passed out.

Van RALT directed MOSSOP to drive to a nearby wood where the former stuck her into a hollow tree and left her there. It was allegedly stated that she would come to her senses the following day and the men returned to Kenilworth. There was and still remains a public house in Hagley called the Lyttleton Arms, which was located on the main Kidderminster to Birmingham Road. More latterly with road enhancements, the public house now sits on a side road. The logical route back towards Kenilworth from the public house would have been through Clent, to Bromsgrove, and thence into Warwickshire. This route is the opposite direction to the wooded area on the main Birmingham Road where the deceased was recovered.

It would appear that there was a link between Van RALT and an act appearing at the Coventry Hippodrome in 1938, the performers being known as 'Frick and Frack' however the grounds for such a link is undefined. Checks of the nationality database subsequent to 1948 (probably in 1953 following the disclosure by Mrs HAINSWORTH) identify two Van RALT nominals.

The first is Pieter Van RAALT who landed in 1948, and had an address in London SE25, the second was a female who held a permanent address in London but occupied a teaching position in Nottingham. Significantly, the female, Laura Frances Ryllis Van RAALTE had on 17th August 1940, vacationed in Malvern staying at the Beauchamp Hotel, and thus has arguably some relationship with Worcestershire. There is nothing on the file to indicate whether it was possible in 1954 to establish whether Ms Van RAALTE was still alive, however there is a report concerning the individual using the present tense which would seem to indicate that in 1954 she was still surviving. If one is to take the post mortem report of Professor WEBSTER as being precise, then in 1940, Ms Van RAALTE was over forty years of age and would just about fall outside the requisite parameters for the deceased.

LINES OF ENQUIRY

NOMINATION OF SUSPECTS

Following the disclosure by Hainsworth, Jack Mossop and Van Raalte appear to be worthy of review. If taken at face value, there are a number of factors, which would key in with the information known. Unfortunately it is now extremely difficult to clearly identify the degree of information which was released into the public arena which would allow for the story to be sewn together by Hainsworth. In relation to the area of Hagley, Hainsworth may have had a degree of knowledge. When making the disclosure she was resident in Claverly, a small Shropshire village lying just outside the Wolverhampton conurbation. Hagley in those days would lie on a route between the Warwick, Shrewley areas and Claverly. It would appear that the Public House was quite well-known and was a point to where persons would travel for a day out. It was a waypoint in the general area of Hagley and Stourbridge used as a means of direction or a marker for directions.

REVIEW OF STATUS OF CRIME

The status of the crime as an unsolved murder is based considerably on the post-modern report of Professor Webster, in his field, Professor Webster was regarded as being pre-eminent, however with the passage of time, the Identification of new concepts, and the modification of previously held beliefs may result in a differing perspective being placed upon the cause of death. Exploration of this concept has been undertaken and there is no advantage taking this forward.

WITNESSES

Whilst the only identified witnesses survive, these individuals can only proffer information surrounding the discovery of the remains, some substantial time following the death. Over the passage of time no other witnesses have been identified despite the factor that the death was broadcast nationally in an investigative style programme by John Stalker. The prospect of locating witnesses at this juncture is remote.

MEDIA APPEALS/COMMUNICATIONS STRATEGY

The prospect of receiving information, which would move the enquiry forward following a general media appeal, is minimal. Indeed the prospect is that the appeal would generate considerable interest from the perspective of obsessionalist, theorists and individuals as archived in the rear of the folder. The opportunity of working with an investigative journalist who seeks to undertake a programme or a part programme concerning the case is rather more appealing. This would potentially facilitate a mechanism of re awakening the public awareness, and those having genuine knowledge prompted to be in touch. That said, the case was subject to a television programme produced by John Stalker, broadcast nationally, which resulted in no additional material being forthcoming.

ARREST STRATEGY

The passage of time, the demise of MOSSOP and the hitherto non-identification of Van Raalte who would now be in the latter phase of this life, if indeed he has not predeceased this report. At this time there are no other potential offenders identified, thus an arrest is not envisaged.

SEARCH STRATEGY

The passage of time has rendered impractical a search otherwise than in the event of the identification of a potential offender. It is highly likely that even after the passage of time, that the offender would maintain either media reporting or similar, and thus would be the subject of the search.

INTERVIEW STRATEGY

The interview strategy at this stage cannot be defined, but in the unlikely event of a suspect coming to notice this would be developed.

IDENTIFICATION STRATEGY

Identification of the deceased after this passage of time is somewhat difficult. There may well be opportunities to be explored in respect of DNA profiling and thereby gain a lineage match. Extensive enquiries to identify the resting-place of the remains have thus far failed. An interment would have taken place, however it is unclear as to where the remains would be buried, and where the ownership of the remains lies.

FORENSIC STRATEGY

Consideration has been afforded to the use of the expertise of a Forensic Archaeologist, Forensic Anthropologist, Forensic

Environmentalist, Palaeontologist and an Odentologist. Additionally, the advances in DNA techniques have been researched The Forensic Archaeologist may have been able to assist had there been any photographs of the scene recorded. At this stage I am unable to identify whether this was the case. Most certainly there is no record of such on the file. The scene has decayed over the passage of time as indeed has the tree, and thus no scene worthy of calling such remains. The identification of the deceased has a potential to move the enquiry forward. This can potentially be achieved by virtue of DNA analysis of the remains, and extraction of the mitacondrial DNA. Furthermore the origins of the deceased could potentially be ascertained through analysis of the bone constituents thereby providing supportive structure to the assertions of Hainsworth. The final resting-place of the bones has yet to be ascertained. In such cases, the remains were buried in a 'paupers' grave. Enquiries with the cemeteries within the Stourbridge and surrounding West Midlands's area have failed to identify the resting-place of the deceased. Thus without source material such forensic initiatives are flawed.

CONCLUSION

At this stage with the passage of time, there are no clear investigative leads. If the location of the remains were established, development of the DNA processes has not afforded investigative opportunities. Any person involved, if surviving, would be in excess of eighty years of age and the prospect of a prosecution would at best be remote.

I therefore make the following recommendations:

- The case is identified as being closed,
- Consideration should be afforded to placing the documentation in the Worcestershire Records Office as an historic document.

13 July 2005

I Nicholls, Detective Chief Inspector

ADDENDUM

As per attached e mail communication between DCI NICHOLLS and DCS ALBUTT on 28th July 2005, this file has now been declared closed and is not for henceforward to be regarded as a live investigation.

28 July 2005

I. Nicholls

Detective Chief Inspector

NON FICTION FROM APS PUBLICATIONS
(www.andrewsparke.com)

Aramoana (Andrew Sparke)
Beating The Banana: Breast Cancer and Me (Helen Pitt)
Bella In The Wych-Elm (Andrew Sparke)
Changing Lives: The Leaps and Bounds Method (Horsfall & Sparke)
Croc Curry & Texas Tea: Surviving Nigeria (Paul Dickinson)
Dub Poets In Their Own Words (Eric Doumerc)
Food and Cancer Prevention (Andrew Sparke)
Indie Publishing: The Journey Made Easy (Andrew Sparke)
Istanbul: The Visitor Essentials (Andrew Sparke)
More Swings Than Roundabouts: The Life of Carlos 'Robin' Medina (John Wright)
Piggery Jokery In Tonga (Andrew Sparke)
Rear Gunner(Andrew Sparke)
Stutthof (Andrew Sparke)
The Strange Free-Fall Of Fred Ryland (Helen Pitt)
The Ways Of Mevagissey (Andrew Sparke)
Tithes & Offerings (Rebirtha Hart)
War Shadows (Andrew Sparke)
What I Think About When I Think About Aikidoo (Mark Peckett)
Your Kid and Crohn's: A Parent's Handbook (William Sparke)

PHOTOGRAPHICS
Images (Andrew Sparke)
Istanbul In Pictures (Andrew Sparke)
Wild Life (David Kiteley)
Shapely Curves and Bumpers (Lee Benson)
Elsewhere (Joanna Leszczynska)

36246826R00037

Printed in Great Britain
by Amazon